SOUTHERN MESSENGER POETS

DAVE SMITH, *Editor*

Also by T. R. Hummer

Bluegrass Wasteland: Selected Poems, 1982–2001 (2004)

Useless Virtues (2001)

Walt Whitman in Hell (1996)

The 18,000-Ton Olympic Dream (1991)

Lower-Class Heresy (1987)

The Passion of the Right-Angled Man (1984)

The Angelic Orders (1980)

Translation of Light (1976)

THE INFINITY SESSIONS

poems

T. R. HUMMER

Louisiana State University Press
Baton Rouge

Manufactured in the United States of America
First printing

Designer: Amanda McDonald Scallan
Typeface: Whitman
Printer and binder: Thomson-Shore, Inc

Library of Congress Cataloging-in-Publication Data

Hummer, T. R.
The infinity sessions : poems / T. R. Hummer.
p. cm. — (Southern messenger poets),
ISBN 0-8071-3055-9 (cloth : alk. paper) — ISBN 0-8071-3066-4 (pbk. : alk. paper)
I. Title. II. Series.
PS3558.U445I54 2005
811'.54—dc22

2004022549

The paper in this book meets the guidelines for permanence and durability of the Committee on Production Guidelines for Book Longevity of the Council on Library Resources. ♾

For Theo and Jackson

His fate is like that of the unfortunate victims whom the tyrant Phalaris imprisoned in a brazen bull and slowly tortured over a steady fire; their cries could not reach the tyrant's ears so as to strike terror into his heart; when they reached his ears they sounded like sweet music.

—KIERKEGAARD

CONTENTS

III

RAIN DOWN RAIN

Suite for Mabel Louise "Big Maybelle" Smith, 1924–1972

IV

MEDICINE FOR A NIGHTMARE

Suite for Sun Ra (Herman Poole "Sonny" Blount), 1914–1993

V
THE CHAOS REMASTERINGS

VI
LIVES OF THE ANGELS

ACKNOWLEDGMENTS

Titles of all poems in certain sections of this book are song titles from albums, as follows:

"For Dancers Only: Suite for Jimmie Lunceford, 1902–1947": titles from *Jazz Portraits: Jimmie Lunceford and His Orchestra, 1935–1944,* Sarabandas 1993.

"Nobody's Sweetheart: Suite for Adrian Rollini, 1903–1956": titles from *Adrian Rollini—Bouncin' in Rhythm,* Pavilion Records Ltd. 1995.

"Rain Down Rain: Suite for Mabel Louise 'Big Maybelle' Smith, 1924–1972": titles from *Big Maybelle: The Complete OKeh Sessions 1952–1955,* Legacy's Rhythm and Soul Series, 1994.

"Medicine for a Nightmare: Suite for Sun Ra (Herman Poole 'Sonny' Blount), 1914–1993": titles from *Sun Ra: The Singles,* Evidence Records 1994, and *Monorails and Satellites,* Evidence Records 1992.

Some of these poems have appeared in various magazines, as follows:

Ascent: "After, In the Silence" (as "In the Silence")
The Atlanta Review: "Vapor" (as "Steam"), "Random," "Cancerous" (as "Desperate")
Atlantic Monthly: "Junk Mail"
Brilliant Corners: "Nobody's Sweetheart: Suite for Adrian Rollini, 1903–1956" (11 poems); "Medicine for a Nightmare: Suite for Sun Ra (Herman Poole 'Sonny' Blount), 1914–1993" (11 poems)
Blackbird: "For Dancers Only: Suite for Jimmie Lunceford" (11 poems)
Call: "The Woman," "The Prisoners," "Needing," "Gnosis," "The Kabbalist"
Kenyon Review: "Zero," "Years," "X," "The Universe," "After"
Image: "Having," "Either"
Salt: "Rain Down Rain: Suite for Mabel Louise 'Big Maybelle' Smith" (11 poems)

For encouragement, information, and pointed critique, the author owes thanks to David Baker, Sascha Feinstein, Garrett Hongo, and Philip Levine.

THE INFINITY SESSIONS

THE INFINITY SESSIONS

In the sealed room, a spotlight switches on.
Silence. Processed atmosphere. The cynosure reveals
An enormous microphone

Hung in the middle of the air, blue steel
And diamond in this illumination,
Impervious, suspended from nothing visible.

It is an act of faith to imagine
The equipment it portends, firmaments
Of co-ax and junctions foregrounding the great Machine

With its light-years of tape, slide-switches, input
Jacks in countless ranks, vast monitors
Arrayed behind tinted panes and laminated plates

Of something crystalline, denser
Than any glass. And beyond, at the controls,
A nebulous dark shape: the Engineer?

Does he give a signal? No matter. Enter the souls,
Stage right, of the players. They surround
The microphone. They lift and hold

Their horns. In the darkness, without a sound,
The relays close; the tape slides by.
What will it be this time? Shuffle for the lovers found

Dead in an alley? Ballad for the boy
Who slipped over the edge? Nobody wants to call
The song. But this is fate. No mercy

In this business, the musicians know. They all
Lived and died for it, common names forgotten.
But note by note, take by take, their lyrical

Stumbling fattens the vault of heaven.
Omniscience has a lot to answer for. The seraphic reels spin,
Blues etched wave by wave on the shell of one electron.

And then the great remastering: variations in the key of pain.

I

FOR DANCERS ONLY

Suite for Jimmie Lunceford, 1902–1947

Lunceford's band was one of the finest orchestras of the swing era, its well-drilled sound and the precision of its section playing being unrivalled by any other group. Lunceford's reluctance to pay for additional singers and dancers to tour with his band led to his musicians doing this themselves, and earning the nickname "the performing seals."

—BBC RADIO 3, *100 Jazz Profiles*, "Jimmie Lunsford" (http://www.bbc.co.uk/radio3/jazz/profiles/jimmie_lunceford.shtml)

’TAINT WHAT YOU DO

When the muttering starts in the street, the word *aubade*
Is not in its vocabulary, though freight trains drum their cargo
Of copper wire and emptiness over the river bridge
Straight for the heart of the sun. Some of its timbre is friction,
Wind against brick, iron against asphalt, old rain
Making its way through pipe; some of it is chemical—
Carbon bonding with oxygen, wood and stone breaking down;
Some is irreducible, like dark matter, like the reason
This old man slumps on a rotting stoop, counting
The nickels in his hand and moaning. Morning
Refuses to hear him. Morning has its own game going
And stops at nothing, cruising crosstown to the Horizon Club
In a slick limo, almost silent, anxious to make the drop.

BLUES IN THE NIGHT

The horoscope says disaster is coming. The weatherman
Says rain. Garbage trucks go about their dirty business
Not caring either way. What message did you want
To leave? Who did you say was calling?
There are traditions for such things. One of them says
There is no tradition; it's been saying so forever.
Another says the form repeats itself; just stick around.
Music needs no subject, but one always turns up
Unexpectedly, dragging its trashy story,
A human figure, a woman, her dress black under streetlights.
Look at her: she just got off a bus from nowhere,
Her face shining with sweat. Or has the storm rolled in?

UPTOWN BLUES

All style, all surface—no tears in the harp, no tears in the harpist.
Nothing comes up. Under the Salvation Army awning
They pass an empty hat from hand to hand
Until somebody steals it; slick as a plunger-mute lick,
It disappears. A scum of powdered eggs for breakfast,
Boiled coffee, something that used to be a wedge of bread.
No sermon, no praise, no blame. Everything is forgiven.
The airshafts to the depths are locked. A Sterno drinker
Swallowed the key at midnight, and in the smoggy breaking
Of another backstreet morning, he is sifting his own shit.

WELL, ALL RIGHT THEN

Another morning of broken storefronts, another evening of fists.
By midnight the street is littered with ticket stubs and empties—
Enumerations of emanations, .22 casings, tire carcasses, and fog.
Music at a distance. Lazy jump blues, horns and a shouter;
Streetcar squeals like trombone overtones. By the shuttered door
Of an abandoned smoke shop, two denizens of the lesser order
Of Thrones or Dominations toss pennies at a crack in the sidewalk.
Time on their hands, they loiter in conspicuous violation
Of universal law and normative moral intuition.
Theirs is neither power nor glory. Theirs is the holy boredom
That hovers like incense over the hierarchies of creation.
No cause for alarm. Brass knuckles are redundant here. Snap
Your fingers forever on the backbeat, never on the one or the three.

MARGIE

Things turn ugly. Call it the entropy of beauty.
Just when the dance gets hot, somebody flashes a knife.
Just when the night sky emerges moonless from the smudge
Of twilight, a siren sounds and everyone goes under.
In the dark, *O Jesus* is the password. You said it, pal.
When the lights come on: blood on the sheets.
Come out of the closet with your blackjack
And your bottle of bleach. It's time for the wedding,
Time for the score to settle. Remember how we felt
When the trumpets lifted and riffed the midnight golden?
That moment sublimity burned its mark on our foreheads
And left us for dead. There's nothing now
But to wait for the hit man to show his decorous hand.

BABY WON'T YOU PLEASE COME HOME

Because the telephone can't ring, she ignores the pistol in the closet.
She stays away from the bottle of pills, refuses to walk over the bridge.
Moment to moment, she considers what time feels like, passing
In and out of the alveoli, around and through the aorta.
It has ground glass in it, the finest abrasive brume.
The gibbous moon lays a sharp quadrangle on her bedroom floor—
She studies its boundaries intently. Light here, dark there. Just so.
Perfect, as though God etched it with his carpenter's right angle.
The moon itself: off center, busted, color of a half-healed scab.
God's hands are filthy. But that piano with its crystal riffs—
On the radio it sounds so clean it could almost be a life.

TWENTY-FOUR ROBBERS

Dispossessed is one way to put it. They broke in and took everything.
The story arrives like music from a Victrola smothered
With a fat silk pillow: muted. Somebody somewhere saw it.
Somebody else knew the driver. There were hacksaws and lockpicks,
Rumors of a pistol-whipping. Suddenly there was silver
On the pawnshop counter, bracelets and wedding rings.
Redistribution of wealth. Somebody drank a gimlet
At the corner bar and paid with a double sawbuck.
It was Robin Hood in a zoot suit. It was Ali Baba sliced in half.
They were having a party in the Avenues, Mardi Gras in June.
Cabs rolled in from the Boroughs. *That's my steak knife.*
Where'd you get that garter? Soup kitchens shut down early.
Posters of Marx appeared on the fence of the vacant lot:
TO EACH ACCORDING TO HIS NEED. In the middle of a chorus
Somebody screaming: *Open sesame. Open sesame . . .*

I'M GONNA MOVE TO THE OUTSKIRTS OF TOWN

Out this window on a moonless night, she can imagine
There might be a horizon, and the stars must know about it—
That's why they never stop moving. If she had the quick slide-arm
Of a trombone player, she could reach beyond the dark
She knows is a warehouse wall to take hold of it,
And that edge would cut her in half. That's the size of it.
The stations of her days are marked with pots of beans,
Plates of rice, the way the tired men lean on their elbows, eating.
They stink, but they have jobs. If an assembly line were long enough
It could stretch beyond the projects to some countryside
Where an unimaginable pastoral unfolds as far as the ocean,
Containing cows, perhaps, containing birds, containing trees.
Pack your bags, sweetheart. Or, screw it—just send for your things.

FOR DANCERS ONLY

The scavengers of twilight turn up with almost nothing—
A lipstick tube, a broken saxophone reed—
And, for their trouble, the Captain breaks their thumbs.
What it takes to earn a living: get it right or not at all.
Get it from schoolboys on the street, Sign of the Horse,
Plastic bag of powder ten bucks, five bucks, one.
Supply and demand. Location. Profit margin.
Or are you just another dreamer, like your mother's cousin
Who thought he could sing? He ended up,
Where was it again? In an alley? At the bottom of the ocean?
Learn the moves. Don't step on any toes.
Have you got the beat? Give me your hand. I'll lead.

LE JAZZ HOT

The finger of God comes down like whatever you care to call it—
Storm, or flame, or a chemical bolt of indifference—
What counts is the gesture, the color of light, the scar.
A sharkskin suit and wingtips in the closet.
A garter belt and a condom in the bureau drawer.
Conditions keep changing, one moment all essence,
The next all shit, and everything in between.
The snapshot on the table is heartless; you see in the eyes
Of the woman that she knows what ending means.
Closure is a crack in the chest like a rim shot,
Syncopation of stop-time, a diminished chord in the brain.

THE LONESOME ROAD

The black cars move in their endless funeral line.
Somebody's on his way, going, going, gone—
Not *home* but *back*. Not *passed away* but *shattered.*
Black limousines like notes on a staff, hearse
Like a big bass clef. The tuba player lifts his load
Of dented brass at graveside. He blows
Three great dark notes, a minor triad.
Why is he always early? *The good,* he thinks,
They all die young. But when will the drummer show
With his bell and his snappy snare? He can't remember
Driving here, or where this big horn came from—
Only the music in the parlor, *O Didn't He Ramble*
On the gramophone. That, and the syncopation
Of tires on asphalt. Odor of alcohol, texture of felt,
Distant flavor of brass. That, and the cold counterpoint
Of a stethoscope on his chest. Breath out of tune, out of time.

II

NOBODY'S SWEETHEART

Suite for Adrian Rollini, 1903–1956

Adrian Rollini was the greatest bass saxophonist of all time, one of the first jazz vibraphonists, and a talented multi-instrumentalist who could make music on such novelty instruments as the "hot fountain pen" (a miniature clarinet with a saxophone mouthpiece) and a "goofus." . . . [H]e played piano and xylophone as a youth, performing Chopin at the Waldorf Astoria when he was four. After joining the California Ramblers in 1922, it was suggested that Rollini learn the potentially cumbersome bass sax; it only took him a week.

—SCOTT YANOW, *All Music Guide*

BEATIN' THE DOG

It's a shame how things go down. At the end
Of the endless ball, the lovers pack their lovely gear
And split. A shame how the man in the tux
Smooths his moustache with his thumb
While the woman he came in with adjusts
Her straps and hisses *Screw you, Jack, I'm a lady.*
A shame how God bends starlight through the crystal
Windshield of the Buick where the woman spits
A little blood and the man reconsiders
The bruise on the back of his hand. God
Keeps score in a tiny notebook. The deadly sins
He totals glissando towards infinity. People leave
Their lives this way; God notes it down
As pure information, along with the name
Of the last tune the band was playing
As the lights came up and the dancers
Remembered each others' tapped-out faces
While the piano staggered and mumbled
Christ, what a holy living shame.

SWING LOW

It's a harsh dawn that makes its way through the transom
Into the parlor where the woman, passed out on a couch,
Covers her eyes and goes on dreaming. It's a cruel siren wail
That makes her grind her head into the velvet pillow, groaning.
In the bathroom down the hall, her sister brushes her weeping hair.
In the bedroom, their mother sits stunned. This is the house
Brushed by the wing of the desolate angel. The news is full of it,
How the fierce seraph smote them—there's even a photograph.
Never mind the flame-studded mace, how high he swung it—
Consider the eyes, their desperate metaphysical glow.
You'd swear the creature was terrified. You'd think he was driven
To his own destruction. But when the arm came down:
Not a subtone of mercy in it. And look at them now,
Broken, soulless, adrift in inevitable light
As ferries break dark water, sounding dissonant horns.

ARKANSAS BLUES

Long way from the nest, the starlight flickers on the doorknob.
Don't be a stranger—write, the beer trucks rattle.
It's not about sentiment. It's about being dead broke and worthless
In a place where even cops don't care if they know your name.
There's a cemetery at the end of the street; children play there
All day Sunday. What kind of world is that? You can hear them singing
Songs that would make a fiddler's hair stand on end.
They're dancing on graves. They're knocking angels down.
Somewhere the wrath of God is looking for its big black belt,
But nobody paid the light bill, the current's off,
The closet of Heaven is dark as a moonless midnight.
Time to hoist a can of beans, time to hop a freight.
The horizon's not that far away, and it looks like home.

FEELIN' NO PAIN

An informal feeling comes, everything said
In simple rhyme. *Moon. June. Spoon.*
You can count on those. Beyond, all seriousness aside,
There's the fog of the anesthetic, the scalpel's margin.
Somebody's blowing a note so low
Only whales can hear it. It goes on all afternoon
Like a house party in hell: you just don't know
You're being punished. But you'll remember soon.

A MUG OF ALE

In the old country things were never like this.
Men wore ties while they shoveled shit.
They called you *sir* while they pounded your face with a brickbat.
On this bloody continent you get no bloody respect.
The parlors are ugly, the pigeons are dirty and sad.
God struts around with a big diamond ring and a hip flask.
He loves the music but he never tips the band.
Watch out for him and his crew. They'll burn you blind
With a lightning bolt, then buy the house a round.

HONOLULU BLUES

Sleet the color of peat smoke blows in from the dying lake
With its sizzle-cymbal strut and harmonic of garbage.
Been living here too long. And too long gone.
The monotone of the sunset jangles like a drawn
Slide note on a hokey lap-steel. Some places men
Line up against walls and wait for other men to shoot them.
Here, nobody bothers. The swing shift whistle
Is judgment enough. How long has it been
Since you drowned in forty fathoms of pure lagoon?
A place you can't get to from here—another life, another planet.
The men against the wall are frozen there.
Someone brings them a turquoise drink with a paper umbrella.
When the carbines start to riff, they don't even seem to hear.

IT HAD TO BE

There's a future in it for someone. Every time the light
Shifts, there's a fortune foretold. The fated nature
Of the thunderbolt, the randomness of the bullet:
Whoever can read it wins. The wheel plays a little
Ragtime ditty as it spins on its brass axle:
She gets a fistful of twenties, he gets hit by a bus.
This bar is full of losers, but the music is classy.
You could sit here all night and hardly feel alone
If you can stand the relativity. Just as the saxophone
Hits a certain low note, the neon flickers.
It means something to somebody somewhere.
The slot machine by the men's room shoots its load.

SAVAGE SERENADE

At the end of the alley they are cooking bones in a pot.
What else is there to do on a Sunday afternoon?
The churches have locked their doors; the bars won't open
For hours. It smells like ammonia, gelatin, burning hair.
It's the color of a tarnished saxophone. The bass harmonica
Somebody swiped from a pawnshop gurgles in the background.
He wants to play a melody on it, *O Susanna* or *Dixie,*
But the enormous instrument resists him, spewing
Nothing but atonal subsonics, until another man smacks him
Upside the head with a rolled-up magazine.
A quick fight breaks out. The harmonica's a decent blackjack.
The magazine lies forgotten in a carton: *National Geographic.*
On the ripped cover, a photo of aboriginal peoples
Living quiet lives on a distant continent. There's trouble
In the inner palace, revolution on the far side of the moon.
Someone passes a dipper of soup. Someone sniffs it and refuses.
The cold-cocked man wakes up and chokes it down.

NOBODY'S SWEETHEART

Don't believe it. It's not that anyone lied—
The problem is deeper. It has to do with God,
You might as well say, or with the meaninglessness
Of this particular language. He puts his affairs
In order, meticulously, saying nothing to anyone.
Or: she does something unspeakable with a kitchen knife.
We see these things hazily, through an unfocused lens.
But the music on the radio comes through clearly,
A jazzy little hopped-up waltz. Pretty. It sings *Don't worry.*
At least there's one perfect tune the dead can dance to.

LUCKY LITTLE DEVIL

Forget the new Roadmaster, forget the slick wingtips,
Fat money clip, Zippo, pinky ring.
Stripped down, he's a washrag, a sack of rusty wrenches,
A plucked monkey with a bootlicker's crooked grin.
Under the light, his skin is the color of gruel,
Grainy as newsreel, the birthmark over his heart
Black as a cartoon bullet hole. Forget the shadow.
Forget the loaded dice, the smuggled gin.
He's otherworldly now in the altogether.
Bring on the alcohol, bring on the sterile blade.
On a good day, he would have pistol-whipped his mother.
He's rehabilitated. He's ready to dirge and drain,
He's high-rolling toward the oven and the urn.

AFTER YOU'VE GONE

There'll be a difference in the moonlight,
Something missing, something added
The color of the track a neutrino cuts
Through heavy water in a mineshaft.
There'll be a sentimental re-sorting
Of all detritus: locks of hair, humus, grit,
Photographs of strangers dancing,
Refugees at a distant border
Leaning on each other, locked
In someone's exhausted arms.
That, and a spell of deadening repetitions:
The bass line of planets revolving,
Dark-toned as the dirty chemistry
That revises you, sums you up.

III

RAIN DOWN RAIN

Suite for Mabel Louise "Big Maybelle" Smith, 1924–1972

With the uncanny ability to be a fist-shaking, house-rocking vocal flamethrower . . . [and] frustrated by love and life, Maybelle poured her heart into the performance of every song. . . .

—liner notes, *Big Maybelle: The Complete OKeh Sessions 1952–1955*

MY COUNTRY MAN

Hoe-chop and axe-fall. Night, and the big voice grows.
Moonlight on galvanized barn roof. Wind over cutter-bar and cow.
Somebody owns this wasteland of rusted-out pickups
And leg irons. This ruined jail: somebody holds the deed.
In culverts under bridges, whole villages lie sleeping,
Children piled in muddy eddies, mothers washed away.
Somebody's in charge of the pig farm and the stink
Of the paper mill. All night chainsaws rehearse
Their clutched melisma in the piney woods, and the moon
Revolves its doomed searchlight in the sky.
You'll never find him. He's always where you aren't,
Changing his keys and his signatures, breaking your idiot heart.

RAIN DOWN RAIN

Soaks into humus, backs up against the turn row,
Rips in a quick meander through the middle of the bridge.
In the sheet-metal roadhouse you can't even hear yourself drink.
Leaks over the threshold from the lake of the parking lot,
Seeps into sheetrock, shorts out the neon jukebox, the inevitable
Blues—you already couldn't follow it—breaking down.
Molds feed in the half-empty silo. Enters the abandoned church
Through its ruptured roof, razes the dry-rotted pulpit.
Landscape in a black and white coma like a gelatin-silver print:
Thunder flattens the scene toward an early twilight. Mercy
On the pitch-pine, mercy on the shed, mercy on the tractor tire
And the swelling corpse of the cow. Mercy on the archetype:
Everybody talking, nobody doing a blesséd thing.

WAY BACK HOME

Pastoral? The folk who lived here loaded up their trucks
With the garbage that was their birthright and high-tailed it
North, each a jazz musician or a future rhythm and blues star.
That's as true as saying *How beautiful the copses,*
How gentle-eyed the sheep. The angels know
The destructive power of a myth. When they swept down
To squat in the abandoned shacks and tune the tractors,
No one believed in them. They couldn't get a bank loan.
Pretty soon they too were fronting ferocious swing bands
In the honky-tonks of Kansas City, oh fortunate fall,
The will of God, who booked them there. The story of us all.

SEND FOR ME

Let it be by starlight code or the Rorschach of thunderheads.
Pentecostal lightning will get through even here.
The hedgerows choke with bramble-vines impenetrable as lead,
But radiance will leak past every seam.
Don't let the distance fool you, acres of nothing but acres—
We've been down this dirty tract a thousand times before.
Let it be by cattlegram, the dits and dahs of crows.
The armadillo is your messenger boy, opossum, civet cat, vole.
Send the ticket etched in the ink of cistern water
Hidden in the false bottom of a buzzard's wing.
Whatever you do, sweetheart, do it soon.
We're hypnotized. We're wasted. We won't last here for long.

YOU'LL NEVER KNOW

This place has borders: trailer park, brick plant, drive-in.
It suffers churches, three stores, a motel with a slot machine.
Its exact description depends on your metaphysics:
What weather do you vote for? Which angel gets your laundry clean?
From here it looks subatomic. Just when you understand
How the speed limit works, they change the geography.
The quark in a mayor's suit knows what a force uncertainty is—
Having no mass and a negative charge can set you free.
WELCOME TO THE LOCAL, a billboard reads. DISCOVER YOUR SENSE OF PLACE.
The police chief comes out of the whorehouse. *What a screamer,* he says.

AIN'T NO USE

Hitchhiked or hoboed freight trains. Went on buses. Went by boat.
Walked if they had to. Begged for bread. Got here and found out the truth:
There is work in the crotch of the slaughterhouse, a bed in a cardboard box.
The night streets rumble with garbage trucks—how can you sleep on a bench
When airbrakes squeal and grinding wheels down-clutch into your dreams?
No turning back. The pillar of flame brakes into a pillar of salt.
And no use praying. God lives uptown in the middle of the block
With a cane and a can and an old blues harp, tunes a penny a shot.
For another penny he'll do a dance, for a nickel the second verse.
It's all the same wherever you go, but some places it's even worse.

YOU'LL BE SORRY

The wreck of a tractor rusts in an empty lot
Behind the abandoned laundry, across from the burnt hotel.
Somebody pulled the plug and this whole side of town
Flicked off. Pigeon in the mailbox. Skunk on the cornice, scrambling.
No ghosts. The dead never had a deed here. They're evicted—
Their ectoplasmic junk tossed on the sidewalk, exorcised.
The landlord torched the building while the band was tuning up
In the parlor off the lobby, O miserable ballad of essences,
Angelic body of smoke with a guitar hidden in it,
Useless siren, useless song, the working girls of the provinces
Lit up at last, divas riffed in firelight against the stars.

DON'T LEAVE POOR ME

They know where the angel hides: in the other closet
At the back of the house, where greasy overalls molder
And newspapers rot into gnostic dust. The angel is easy.
Money is different. Its lineaments vanish
Like piano chords into air. It hides its radiance.
If they pray, they get the angel—his mothballed magnificence
Shuffles into the kitchen with a checkerboard and a stool.
But the deus absconditus of the checkbook is untouchable,
Mystical, cool. Rain down, great mercy. Manifest. Shake this house.
They bear the ark of emptiness, they mumble the nameless name.
Like a grand opening at a pawnshop: no merchandise so far,
Just a stack of blank tickets and a universe of desire.

NEW KIND OF MAMBO

In front of the church, a Nativity scene, camels and a lonely donkey;
By the library door a crumbled lion, a plaque, and a Civil War mortar.
At the bootlegger's house, a squad car. The sheriff gets his Sunday fifth
And a grocery sack of dollar bills with the gift of a fried fish sandwich.
At midnight the music of the spheres stumbles and changes key.
Christmas Eve: granted the gift of words, the camels tell pointless jokes
While the Buddhist lion resigns himself to the seedy passion of the donkey.
The sheriff grins at his flashlight. He knows the shifting of the gyres
Is nothing a riot gun can't handle. Nobody leaves the scene.
In the grocery bag, in his newspaper robes, the greasy fish is speechless:
The rough beast has a nightstick now, and bellies up to the killing floor.

OCEAN OF TEARS

Start walking. It's a long way to the crossroads,
Long way to the roadhouse, long way to Easy Street.
Around here, the pastures are going bankrupt,
The stock market of the cornfield crashes and burns.
Take a look around, then wave goodbye.
Nobody cares what happens when the drainage ditch
Where you launched your navy collapses, or the copse
Of scrub oaks you prayed in goes under the wrecking ball.
Acre by acre this landscape sputters and darkens.
Nothing left but the cutting of losses. Liquidation. The bottom line.
It's filthy with salt, the water rolling in. Fathoms deep. It stinks.
You've still got time to disappear, but it's too late for an ark.

THE OTHER NIGHT

Emptied out now, as after the Rapture,
Or postapocalyptic. You can call and call,
You can scream a chord: no angel will answer.
Not a particle of your childhood remains,
No gravestone or broke-back ruin of your desire.
It's wiped up now, sucked into tornadic vacuum,
Clean and lean as the surface of a proton.
And it's not so bad, no genealogy, no story—
You're nobody anyway, and you always were.
The new darkness is not unkind, however unholy—
It's comforting, the mythless sky without stars,
Your clarified position in a stripped geometry.
What breaks your heart is the music: choirs
Without blue notes, vanished syncopation,
The squareness, a deadbeat purity.

IV

MEDICINE FOR A NIGHTMARE

Suite for Sun Ra (Herman Poole "Sonny" Blount), 1914–1993

[A]t the heart of everything that Sun Ra did or said was the claim that he was not born, that he was not from earth, that he was not a man, that he had no family, that his name was not what others said it was. . . . Sometimes he said he had no mother; or he implied that he was from Saturn; and by evading dates . . . he became ageless and timeless. "You can't ask me to be specific about time," he said. "Me and time never got along so good—we just sort of ignore each other."

—JOHN F. SZWED, *Space Is the Place: The Lives and Times of Sun Ra*

MEDICINE FOR A NIGHTMARE

Manifesto: cosmic infarction. Rx: dynamite cure.
Telegram: build a spaceship big enough to hold
Two infinities, one female, one male.
The Rosicrucians of Birmingham are gathering
White noise in a quicksilver sack.
In the next room: barbecue, sulfur smoke,
Whiskey, and a kick-ass big band.
Through crystal portals in the turrets
The subtlest radiations enter.
The real is out there somewhere.
It has glowing rings. It's vast.
It spins like a Sufi on methedrine.
It has presence and grace but no mass.
A man robed in tinfoil holds a mirror,
A woman fronts a bullet microphone.
It's time to decide. It's time to defend
The essences. Light the fuse and let it roll.

SATURN

The most ordinary things up here are the most unreal.
This hangover is an illusion, like the memory of the man
Who pistol-whipped, or the blade woman and the story of the scar.
It's impossible that what presents itself inside these starry rings
As *fact* is anything at all. You have to unbelieve just to get
Your sorry ass out of bed in the morning and moan. You have to lean
In front of the mirror and smack your forehead until it bleeds.
Who stands in the grace of the firmament? Who knows what they think
They know? *Once on a train I journeyed . . . once in a gutter I stank.*
Remember the sound of your mother's heart in the universe of the womb?
You were drowning then and you're drowning now, you without a name
Or a fine silk suit or a cigarette or a planet to call your own.
You're a packet of gasses without a face, you're a singing hologram.

MESSAGE TO EARTHMAN

Cablegram: turned up at the county morgue in a blind rigor
With a dead man's name in mind. Wish you were here.
Send it collect in a radium envelope, return address
The color of platinum dust, person to person, insured,
Return receipt. Let the carrier ride the Schwinn from hell.
This planet is deaf and oblivious. It takes a mighty knock
To rouse some people's interest in their own front door.
Make it mercurial. Offer a handful of beads, a busted mirror,
A smallpox patient's blanket, holy ghost in a cardboard box.
Kansas City flickers like a sick TV, New Orleans is halfway gone.
When they open up, say it's from me. Sing them a birthday song.

ROCKET #9

It's not what you think, and never was. The dark
Grid of a cyclone fence can't describe it,
Or the color of spit on a sidewalk, gilt tin of a snapshot's frame.
It has hooks in time so deep any drummer would die for it,
And has, and will. It has sweep, grace, and an angular momentum
That would rip your shoulder out of the socket
If you tried to grasp it. It's out where anyone can see it—
By the drugstore, in a vacant lot, down a blind alley where a crowd
Of old drunks sleep it off. It's in the back of a cab
On the way to the depot. It's with three junkies, dancing.
It has so much lyric traction that when the old deaf woman
On the street corner puts out her hand, a quarter in her palm,
It's on her in an instant and they're both gone
At the speed of starlight in a two-step shuffle toward heaven.

THE SUN ONE

That was a biblical journey, from siege to city to mirage—
We made the miraculous portage to excavate Babylon
From an overgrown lot in Chicago where dust had filled the throats
Of the lion and the eagle and the socialist, and the temple tumbled down.
We came with chisels and shovels, straight razors and saxophones
To reinvent the universe, ballroom by roadhouse by bar.
That was a devastated horizon, cursed and blistered and choked.
We traveled on foot or by chariot, on a train with a chrome club car.
We'd been branded and aped and orphaned, murdered and urned and dumped—
The blade went through our transparency; we were invulnerable as air.
The brass tunes up in a cattle truck, the bass works its slaughterhouse line.
It's a gift to wake with the light in your face, such brilliance everywhere.

SATURN MOON

A serious fogbank from inland. Cities sock in, shut down.
The ocean groans in a fever all morning, the sky fading nickel steel.
Craters and ridges with Latin names crop up on the courthouse lawn
And the music at Walgreens changes: a raga, an atonal reel.
The old man with musical fillings picks up messages through his teeth.
New dawn, new age, new order. He's heard it all before.
Like some crank on a miserable asteroid calling the police:
You're living on another world. You've been living there forever.
Pointless voices. He tunes them out, just one more dumb mistake.
Even if all they say is true, what difference does it make?

BLUE DIFFERENTIALS

Nobody knows what slips in through the transom of the horizon,
The Egyptian name for the color that refracts in the prism of a horsefly's wing—
Faint tincture of a drowned child's skin, the *n*th distillation of which,
If caught in a bottle and swallowed, would warp your spine into ice.
Whatever it is, it stinks of Armageddon—the moon and the South Pole crashing
Like runaway freight trains under the shocked crotch of Orion,
Mountainous plates of Being shearing off and imploding in the solar wind.
The silence of this midnight sky is insidious illusion, Great Ones.
There's a thrown rod in the engine of the universe, a stripping of the gears.
The old drummer on the sidewalk has the tempo of it. He's beating a paint can,
Sky-flecked. What's on the label? *Cerulean.* He plays his trap of junk
Like a Sherman tank in a wind chime stall, the joyful noise of the brink.

LOVE IN OUTER SPACE

Mostly it's just a big dark room with a swaybacked bed
Shoved under the curtained window. Mostly it's a grim hotel
In a grimy little precinct just this side of the city limits of Pluto.
There's the floating, spacesick and mean. And there's the gravity: zero,
But with the certainty of landfall, knowing you're nothing but freight
Gaining ominous mass inside a ridiculous machine.
Night after night of terrible food, year after year in orbit,
A life on this cosmic chitlin' circuit will warp your gyrocompass.
You pilot by dead reckoning through meteors and asteroid mazes
Staring at the ceiling's constellation of luminous plastic stars.

SKY BLUES

Morning. It's raining in Jersey. This ticket prefigures a train
From here to elsewhere, sure enough, where the sky begins over again
With its microtonal keen of necessity, its emptiness, its free fall
Into a distant century where no animal and no ark
Will cloud the surfaces of certainty with residues of survival.
What makes no sense endures. What goes up in smoke remains.
That's the hope we're left with: blown up, it lasts almost forever
Like the half-life of a busted atom, the solitary trail of a quark,
The silent neutrino that slips through the earth as through a glass of water.

COSMO-EXTENSIONS

Years afterward, everything looks the same: the factory gate,
The warehouse, the rusted-out dump truck. Wouldn't you think
Being dead would matter? But look: there's his father still
In his iceman's coat, always on the verge of lighting out.
There's his mother with her perpetual mantra of worry,
And his brother with his mean right hook, his sister with her asthma.
Went everywhere—Harlem, Saturn, Heaven—and in the end
This is what it comes to: Saturday morning and all the horror of home.
And look at him, if you can find him—hardly there, he's a falling chord,
A fading chorus, chance reverberation, pile of ash
From a fake book somebody used as kindling.
He's an old woman's memory of a Saturday night dance.
Where's the family resemblance now that he's purely ectoplasmic,
Foxfire, chain lightning, swamp gas? They are hands and faces,
They are jobs and crimes of passion, a stack of bills to pay.
He's what he said he was: nondimensional, otherworldly, a cloud
Of diesel smoke from a bus exhaust: gone elsewhere, one way.

HOURS AFTER

Down time in the æther. The parade of the angels dissolves.
They lay down their wings and their trumpets, hang
Their sandals on sky hooks, kick back.
Cheap whiskey and dirty glasses. A ragged pack of cards.
Someone raps a sprung rhumba on timbales. Someone sings.
There's a landlord on the telephone. There's a telegram in the hall.
This one owes. That one's dead. Everyone's hungry. Call home.
A plate of greasy pork chops. A basket of fish and bread.
Lightning. The sign of the absolute. Pick up your bed and walk.
Here comes the Revolution, Apocalypse, the Golden Way.
Earthlings: resistance is futile. Transcendence is a power play.

V
THE CHAOS REMASTERINGS

In Memoriam Robert Olive
citizen, musician, brother
1952–2002

ZERO

Zero balance. Double entry. Every accounting method
Failed. There could be no question of error or ignorance—
His omniscience was intact. But still the recalcitrant numbers,
False sums, disagreement. And the office needed cleaning.
So many outdated records, reports, bits of paper, dust.
It was exhausting to think about. He'd just give up
And go home, if he had one. But even to look out the window,
Where clouds of dark matter accrued and disbursed
And spiral nebulae wobbled unreliably, panicked him.
This was not the job he'd signed on for. There were people
Waiting for results, for the traffic light to change, the cell to divide,
The wounds to numb, the dead to file their forms.

YEARS

Years ago, the story begins. *Once.*
In such-and-such a place, some season or other,
A stranger, two lovers, disaster.
She wants to close the book, but constellations
Of narrative structures interlock: gunfire
In the street, explosions at the embassy,
Betrayal, failure, decades of grinding hopelessness.
How long ago he died, his face pages vanished.
And she, dedicated reader, carries out sentence after sentence,
Her knowledge of the end complete, her execution certain.

X

X is dominant—and fatal. She remembers this
From a poem she read once, in a classroom
Where a shaft of light illuminated dust motes
Levitating over the forehead of a bust of Plato.
But by the teacher's desk, on the blackboard, X
Was the unknown. They found these ideas stunning—
She, Marie, George, and the others—as if knowledge
Were a dangerous mystery. And it was.
But at least there was a classroom. Now
There is only this windowless basement,
One candle, one Bible, one empty bowl,
The sound of bombers overhead, the odor of ozone.
That's it, then—the wind moving like a cripple
Among the leaves? Or slabs of concrete shattered
In the holy crosshairs, blocking the upward portal.

THE WOMAN

The woman on the bus has perfect pitch.
She recognizes an A-flat instantly when it pops
From the squeal of the brakes, and the repeated tonic/flatted fifth,
In concert G, of the ambulance siren. In the hospital room
Little drips and pings arrange themselves on staves
Etched on the back of her eyelids, a pointless postmodern
Score of self-referential repetition, like Philip Glass
On quaaludes. The curse of perfection is not
Losing bits of yourself—it's having no say in the matter.
She would beg for earplugs if she could move her tongue.

VAPOR

Vapor drifts up from the stockpot. He sees beyond
The cloudy window snow still falling apart on the deck,
On the rime-stunned lawn and the blossoms of the tulip tree
Opened too soon, too hopeful. Smell of cooking celery,
Fennel, bouquet garni—weightless, silent, rich. Snowfall,
Snowmelt: the death of the opening blossom, dissevered
By crystal splinters, soundless against mossed brick of the fence.
Sage and champagne vinegar, a little wine. Even the atoms
Are made of something and have to be sweated and stirred:
Far down inside the nucleus, just to the left of the quark—
A little smaller and denser than color or charm, just possible
For God to see if he wears his x-ray glasses—the particle called pain
Chains its cold mutation in the structure of the double helix,
Rising up through the nematode and vole into the foundation stones
Of factories, shops, kitchens of rental houses, releasing the finest haze.

THE UNIVERSE

The universe called him back. Collect. He answered
Several letters, finished all essential reading, distributed
Instructions for his employees, left the building,
And was gunned down by a sniper, or hit by a bus,
Or a piano fell from a chain. He was forever uncertain.
But the way hydrogen atoms excited him, whipped
By the solar wind—about that he could be precise.
It was the particles that wanted him. Their initials
Were etched inside his cells. He returned to the waveforms,
Emptied of himself by fractals and strange attractors.

THREE

Three on the sidewalk: two men in suits
And a woman in a beaded wedding gown.
Family resemblance? Deep in the genes
An altar is raised, a goat sacrificed.
We came on the mainland out of a fogbank suddenly
In our crude boats. We killed all we met
With stones at first, then with their own knives.
Soon there were taxis in scrappy March sunlight,
Little flags on the lampposts, a neon OPEN sign.
The bride is patient. She watches the horizon
For shadows, dust clouds, a tell-tale column of smoke.

SAME

Same street, same car, same yard
She comes home to day after day,
But now she is confused
By the house next door, exactly
Like her house, and the child in a swing,
Exactly like her child. Same moon over the trees—
Her moon?—same hole in the middle of her back.
Nothing for it but to unlock the door,
See what has arrived in the mail,
Read the obituaries. But all the dead
Are like her dead. What can come
After that? Dinner, a conversation,
A quiet game of cards?

RANDOM

Random ritual of constellations: in a dark bedroom,
The man and woman harvest stargas—and out of almost nothing
The new soul starts to flicker. But we must not say it this way.
We avert our gaze. What else is there in the room?
A clock, of course. Digital. It hums its way toward the inevitable—
A bus, a cubicle with a desk, papers, the investigation, the report.
In the beginning you know nothing, then everything is determined
And filed away. Lying on top of the man, tasting his salt, the woman
Makes a mental note of a task that wants completing, something
Somebody said, what to wear to the meeting. And the man,
Almost asleep, sees the face of his dead brother shimmer
In moonlight—where? On a beach? It's important not to know
What the clock is doing, there on the bedside table, ratcheting
Gene after gene out of distant nebulae, finishing its work, retiring.

QUIETLY

Quietly a village rises up in the empty plain,
Then turns instantly into a depressing little city
Where a woman sits at a desk in an ordinary office
Staring at a telephone. It is obvious
That bromeliads and bracken once covered the place
Where her filing cabinets rust—less so that gods
Still swarm around her, gnatlike, unemployed, and pointless.
And when the phone finally rings, she answers it
So discreetly even they are powerless to overhear.

THE PRISONERS

The prisoners put on their orange jumpsuits. They enter
The panel truck single file, take their seats in the eternal order:
Alphabetical. They ride through the winter landscape silently.
In the field beyond the berm where they disembark,
There are trees no one has ever bothered to think of, leafless now
Under a sky where clouds form and re-form and release a patina of snow.
There are bits of paper to be gathered, and cups, and Styrofoam.
There is the perfect skeleton of a rabbit twined with dried ironweed.
That stillness is enviable, that femur, that limestone-colored cranium,
That being impenetrable, never having known the pistol-whip of a name.

OTHER

Other than the blueprint of her hand
There is nothing to hold. Other than
The plumb bob of the afternoon cloud
That settled ten degrees from the horizon.
Other than the whipsaw of memory.
Schematize that, doctors. Give him something
Clear in the compromised blood, in the fog
On the x-ray. Give him the hammer
Of the mind of God. Give him a measure
He can use at the threshold, confused
By unfamiliar dimensions, diminished, other.

NEEDING

Needing a cigarette, he panhandled, but nobody smoked.
Nobody even carried a lighter. Up and down the sidewalk
In front of the newsstand, a crowd of students shuffled,
And workers from the construction site,
And a waiter, and a nurse. It was his strategy
To ask for something else, then mention money.
He'd used it for years, but that repeated *No,*
Sorry, pal, left him speechless. After days of this
The course was clear—first, give up drinking.
Next eating. Next, sit very still in disciplined meditation
Until breathing, too, departs, and God appears.
Then ask God for a smoke. In the desert of your want,
You'll get one—that, and a pillar of salt, a tongue of fire.

MILD

Mild weather, the most difficult to define, ordinary wind,
Ordinary light, only the commonest poisons in the horizon's yellow glow.
This is one of the forms of heat death, she thinks, watching
The man beside her sleep in the transparent afternoon: everything
Averaged out. This is why she wants him—she can fuck him to sleep
So easily on these days without attributes, and see him slip
Into the median. One tree in the garden, one dog in the street,
One snippet of moon in the afternoon sky: multiply these by zero
And you get this dreaming man, naked in a beige motel room.
The mathematic is so miraculous that when he twitches in his sleep
She thinks in love and wonder, don't wake up, you're perfect to me,
You're nothing, nobody, it all adds up to this, stop breathing.

LIFELIKE

Lifelike, the flowers in pots along the pitted street,
The bits of metal scattered among timbers and brickbats
That once were houses and shops, the bodies
Laid out on the sidewalk. This is the art of war,
He thought: make it so real the eye is fooled forever.
This one looks just like a soldier, that one just like a child.
Bombers left gentle brushstrokes in the sky
Beneath which he paused and focused his camera.

THE KABBALIST

The Kabbalist symbols carved on his gravestone reminded him
Of his father, who knew nothing of such things,
But shuffled through God's emanations nevertheless, seeking
The true name of Unconsciousness. That was fine
For his father: when they dragged him home dead drunk,
He attained, his son imagined, the image of the Godhead.
Now, standing watch over his own mound of earth, he reflected
On all his father worked so hard to forget: debt without repayment,
Sin without redemption, the emptiness when they shut the factory down.
Strange how death changes nothing. Meticulous as he had been,
Even beyond the end there were zeroes to be worked off.

JUNK MAIL

Junk mail: opening his credit report, he found the story
Of a woman he'd lied to twelve years before, and a book
He'd lifted from a flea market—a signed first edition—
And the time he'd watched, through a bathroom keyhole, his sister
Touch herself: the Trinity of Credit Bureaus knew his every sin.
He should have been outraged, he should have done—
What? Called the FBI? Filed a lawsuit? Staged an exorcism?—
Whatever you do to foil omniscience. But he kept on reading,
And it went on forever, he couldn't put it down, it was fascinating.

INKSTAINS

Inkstains covered everything: towels, the bathroom floor,
The sink, her body stretched beside the blackened toilet.
Police were baffled. It was as though a whole library
Had emptied its books inside that tiny room.
They searched the house for an answer:
Parlor, kitchen with its meticulous pantry, den
Where a newspaper had coughed up images
Of a burning country and lay blank in the clean lamplight.
But no one found, in plain sight on a bedside table,
The immaculate suicide note written in her own blood.

HAVING

Having refused the transplant, he let his heart wear out,
Then went to the office. Nobody there—a Saturday?
He read the report on the settlement, the recommendation on the lien,
The problematic case of the prostitute's mortgage. Hopeless.
Desire was utterly transparent, like everything now: the window,
Yes, but also the platinum pen set, the stapler, the Xerox machine.
He could barely see his own hands shuffling the reports, signing, filing.
He understood the Stoics now—in resignation, such sweetness.
Memo, he dictated, floating off: *It doesn't pay to borrow.*

GNOSIS

Gnosis of the beetle, anatomy of feldspar,
Quantum structure of the shadow of an oak—
She'd failed all these subjects, and many others.
She regarded her life as a syllabus of repeated disasters,
Muffed true-false questions, bungled essays with such titles
As *God's Customers, Intimate Oceans, Metaphysics of Soap.*
Something in the very nature of knowledge hated her
(She had learned at least that much) and doomed her to repeat
The same exercises and assignments—eternally? Yes,
That would be her punishment: To spend infinity
In one of the Classrooms of Heaven, forbidden
To excuse herself or look out the window, copying her omissions
Into a diamond notebook with a #2 pencil of fire.

FILES

Files full of papers, one dusty window—too high and small
For the dying ficus in the corner—one desk chair,
Cupful of pens, box of paper clips, a photo, rubber bands.
He disposes of certain reports and writes a memorandum.
A courier brings in mail, takes mail away. Lao-tzu,
He remembers, was a bureaucrat. How did he spend his days?
Patrolling the middle path between outbox and inbox?

EITHER

Either the sky was lying, or what was left of his eyes.
The city was just the same—buses, panhandlers,
Ambulances stalking the suburbs. But the stars
Seemed completely rewritten, and the moon
Was swinging back on its hinges like a golden doorway.
Was it really so simple being dead—
His name written in fire beyond the clouds, one step
To take him through the lunar portal?
He turned his back. Where hope and dust conspire,
Either the left hand fills up first, or the right one does.

DREAMING

Dreaming, she found a book she had written
On the rearmost shelf of an abandoned bookstore.
She was not a writer, she had no memory of it,
So bought it out of idle curiosity.
She found her way to a bench in the center of the city
Beside a fountain, and began to read.
Awake, she remembered only the fountain,
The scum of algae on its surface, a rusting coin.
What about the book, demanded her interrogator,
Tightening the thumbscrews and cranking up the voltage.
What was it called? When did you write it
And why? What was its means of subversion?
But the plaza was deserted. There was only a ruined kiosk,
Some bits of shrapnel, and two oily pigeons.

CANCEROUS

Cancerous little town on the brink of a cancerous little sea—
Dark, oily water; dark, oily sky—even the fish, she imagines,
Torn with angry helplessness, pissed on diesel fumes and fog.
That's what this universe is, she thinks: chemotherapy disguised
As a cosmos. But there is music here, an off-key funk. Down the wharf,
A rented ferry floats its American wedding party. Chinese lanterns,
Two saxophones, hors d'oeuvres for every invisible guest. She watches
The bride and groom make one more toast: he, in his dark tux, raising
A skeletal arm, holding the wedding goblet to the delicate skull of his bride.
But no, the watcher thinks, rubbing her eyes, that's an illusion.
She turns her back on the *danse macabre,* dragging her wings and scythe.

BEFORE

Before sleep, sex. Before dinner, a drink,
The evening news. Before that, work. And earlier?
The fossil record, in which certain images glowed
With a half-life that defines the narrative:
Lunch, a meeting, a coffee break,
Back to the moment of his conception.
Before that? Sleep, sex, dinner, the gods cracking down,
Enforcing the eternal silence of the missing links.

AFTER

After the explosion, no one knew what to do
For the boy who'd stood closest to the abandoned leather briefcase.
By some miracle, he was the only one injured. It erupted
In an incense of sulfur and nails as he made his way
To steal it. Holiness has an aura, everyone knows that,
But why would terrorists bother to murder a thief?
The ethics of this question paralyzed everyone in sight
While the boy, unable to breathe, watched God wandering
The station in a business suit, asking occasional strangers
Have you seen my briefcase? There was something urgent in it.

AFTER, IN THE SILENCE

After, in the silence, we understood the depth of our error:
The cosmos was in fact a cabinet of mirrors, the infinity of space
A cheap sleight of hand. The universe was precisely
One billion cubits in duration, encased in a solid dodecahedron of isinglass:
All this designed to distract those who ask too many questions.
Certain stubborn problems vanished. Light moved more slowly
Than we had assumed. It would have washed Manhattan clean
Of bone-dust and ash, but the morning went on precisely as it had to,
There being nowhere else for it to go, and when the three thousand souls
Separated from the vapor of memos and desk chairs, rocked
As they were, together, from our recent illusion, they discovered one mercy
At the center of their loss: The journey to the border would be brief.

VI

LIVES OF THE ANGELS

Duets for Saxophone and Sky

Lester would "just get up and pick up his horn, and sit down, and blow for about an hour." He would announce that he was going to play something pretty, "and he would, and I would tell him how *important* he was, and what a *force* he was in the world, it would never be forgotten, because I don't believe anything's ever lost. . . . I would tell him, 'Your sound will be going round and round and round the world . . . for an eternity.'"

—DOUGLAS HENRY DANIELS, *Lester Leaps In: The Life and Times of Lester "Pres" Young*

For John Kinsella and Michael Dutton

LIVES OF THE ANGELS

Duets for Saxophone and Sky

I. AS GOLDFINCH

Ordinary, ephemeral, skirting shadows at the boundary
Of any little city, he refracts his fragment of a song.
Every note is a manifesto. Sex, food, territory.

Every note is personal. No note is ever wrong.
The price of perfection is that nobody sees it—
Even sunlight is less transparent. All along

The trade routes between hell and points infinite,
The roadhouses of the nebulae fill, vibrate, then empty.
He comes back from the land of the dead even less than spirit.

Nothing changes. You ain't shit, brother. Fly.

II. AS HAWK

The difference is power. The difference is how he can rip.
Fewer notes, but each one takes off a head.
Into the wind he's a black crucifix. With the wind, he sideslips

Across the æther. Even before he was dead
He was like this: shadow of a shadow warrior.
He just refused to know it. Now, transmigrated,

He becomes the symbol of the talon and all it stands for.
Do you think music is easy? The blood on the lip
Of the dying vole is no metaphor:

That disembodied riff from the night sky eats him up.

III. AS WHIPPOORWILL

Of course nocturnal: so many nights the sweet
Choruses hung in midnight cobalt.
And of course *behind* the song, out of sight

In the half moon's smokescreen: whose fault
Was that sideslip, that sudden blue note?
This resurrection is perfect, his true name caught

In the music and its echo, quote and unquote.
Mating habits: hard to see. Life span: indeterminate.
Of course. In this dark who can know? But the smart

Money's all on *short.*

IV. AS BLUEBIRD

This body, though fragile, fits.
The intervals slip easily out of the throat:
Minor third, flat seventh, flat fifth.

Everything now is purpose and light,
Evening air transparent as a glass of everclear.
Sorrow in the music, yes, but hollow bones float

His blueness, a flash in infinity, sheer atmosphere—
Maybe holy, he thinks, but don't quote him on it:
Once back down in nature, he will never

Give it up again for nothing better than heartsick spirit.

V. AS CATBIRD

Why didn't he think of it before?
The song—unending, completely flexible—
Contains everything in this incarnation, a sure

And relentless irony. Within the tiny skull
Of this creature, such chops, such radical inversions,
Everything grist for the riff mill.

Jackhammer, choking cat, foghorn,
He can sound like that: anything impure,
Illegal, destructive, and ugly will be reborn

Wherever he comes to light. Now. Here.

VI. AS BLACKBIRD

And suddenly *this* problem again, the human one,
The constant one, because they always demand it.
Not allowed here. Get out. Leave us alone

With our tuneless malice, our scarecrow spirit.
So the music grows rawer, more inward,
Autumnal. Three are gathered on a fence to play it:

October evening in a freezing rain. Your cabaret card
Is your kinship to the shadow. If a saxophone
Could fly, it would be here, sitting in. *What's the word?*

Blackbird. *What's the price?* If you got to ask, there ain't one.

VII. AS YARDBIRD

Holy one, if you had hands, you could heal your own
Broken wing; if you had words, you could swear
These torturing boys to dust. They are breaking you down

With brickbats and a baseball. This is the future
Of all your singing: against the fence,
Beside the geranium and the plaster gnome, in the corner

Behind the cinderblock house. Incense
Of dogshit. Icon of Masonite. Ruptured condom crown.
They are killing you again, senseless,

Perfect to themselves. Revelation. Genesis. Paradise Blown.

VIII. AS FLOCK OF GRACKLES

Under the extinguished streetlamp, behind the park bench,
Something bright in the half-light. A scattering.
He opens in every direction—inch by inch

Scours the sidewalk, eating. It's a starved business, being
Reborn every second, hundred-headed. He has to gather
Mass. Beetle, bread crust, worm, bits of string,

It's all the same. He is a multitude of hunger.
He contains dissonances, eyes, lice-itch,
Never his own, never not his. Many-hearted, he is after

Not less than everything in the universe, perfect pitch.

IX. AS SKYLARK

All altitude now, he gathers wind; all buoyancy, he burns
In unmitigated sunlight, like a cloud of fire.
No accident, that phrase. If Shelley played saxophone

He'd riff it again altissimo, notes blown higher
Than dogs can hear—Shelley, prophet
Of blues he never heard, Carmichael and Mercer

His hip reincarnations. Does the bird know it—
How the single note ricochets off heaven and turns
Us inside out? Forget that shit.

He's riding with the seraphim, he's golden, he's gone.